Mart

or, The Fair at Richmond

Friedrich von Flotow

(Editor: Glen Carle)

Alpha Editions

This edition published in 2022

ISBN : 9789356909724

Design and Setting By
Alpha Editions
www.alphaedis.com
Email - info@alphaedis.com

Contents

ACT ONE.

(LADY HARRIET, *maid of honor to the queen, has grown listless and pale, refusing to join in the court revels.* SIR TRISTAN, *an old knight, makes love to her; she will have nothing to say to him, and only asks to be let alone. She is tired of her conventional life, and longs for some new and strange adventure. The curtain rises on her richly furnished boudoir.* LADY HARRIET *is lying listlessly on a couch or arm chair, before her dressing table.* NANCY *is putting finishing touches on her mistress' toilet. The ladies in attendance are grouped near the door in center.*)

NO. 1.

CHORUS. Bright as are the stars of heaven,
Sweet as any April flow'r,
Gay of heart, of gentle bearing,
Bless'd with beauty's radiant dower,
Why so sad and pale with languor
Grows thy face, O lovely maid?
Why our friendly circle shunning,
Dost thou sigh alone,
As were some dawning joy delayed?
Every splendid gift of fortune,
All that riches can impart,
Waits upon the maiden's pleasure,
Nothing wins her heart.

(NANCY *takes a bouquet of flowers from one of the ladies and offers it to* LADY H.)

NANCY. See these flowers Sir Tristan sent.

LADY HARRIET (*pushing flowers away*).
I've no heart for lovers' folly,
Every pleasure is at end.

CHO. Bright as are the stars of heaven, etc.

NANCY. Every splendid gift of fortune, etc.

LADY H. Ah, there's naught can win my sad and weary heart.
All your words are vain.

(*Ladies in waiting leave stage.*)

(NANCY *holds hand mirror before* LADY H.)

NO. 2.

NAN. Every heart with love inflaming,
You the Queen's gay court adorn,
Tho' from all a tribute claiming,
Think not love alone to scorn.
Pastimes for your pleasure framing,
We all labor night and day,
Sorrow still your soul is weighing,
All your thoughts to sadness bend,
If I fail in grief allaying,
In its spring your life will end.

LADY H. On my heart 'tis preying, (*she sits up*)
Love, wealth, fame, not weighing,
In its spring time my life will end.
There's naught that charm to life can lend.

(LADY H. *lies back languidly.*)

FOOTMAN (*enters, speaks*). Sir Tristan of Mickleford, Member of the House of Lords, Knight honored—

LADY H. (*interrupting*). We'll spare you the rest.

(*Enter* SIR TRISTAN *with flowers. Bows to the ladies, presents flowers, which* LADY H. *looks at carelessly and drops on table beside her. He is an elderly beau very precise in manner. A few of the ladies return, stealing on the stage to watch the scene, remaining at rear.*)

NO. 3.

TRISTAN (*sings*). Lovely cousin, I implore you,
Hear my suit and do not chaff.
I would say that I adore you—

LADIES (*near door*). He's too civil, though, by half,
He would make a mummy laugh.

(LADIES *leave stage again one by one.*)

TRISTAN. Dare I ask you—

LADY H. Don't be foolish.

TRIS. Dare I ask it you—O dear!
Would you deign—disdain—an offer—

LADY H. For my hand—

NANCY (*aside*). To box his ear!

(LADY H. *laughs aside with* NAN.)

LADY H. Ah, Sir Tristan, he at least can make me smile!

NAN. Ah, Sir Tristan, he at least can make her smile.

TRIS. O, see already she is smiling,
Happy omen, well I know,
O, if mine could be this treasure,
Happy man were I, that's so!

LADY H. Ah, he can all my woe beguile.
What a funny old beau, Ah!
A funny beau.

TRIS. (*speaks*). Fair Cousin, may I ah—dare hope that you—er—will so far condescend to me—uh—uh—as to go for a walk in the park?

LADY H (*indifferently*). Go fetch my fan!

TRIS. (*brings it.* LADY H. *fans violently*). Would it amuse you to—er—er—let us say—go out for a row on the river?

LADY H. (*ignoring him, glances round*). It seems very chilly here. Shut the window—there's a good man!

(TRISTAN *shuts it, trots back to her.*)

TRIS. (*rubbing his hands*). Shall we go hunting, perhaps? It's a capital day for it.

LADY H. (*fans herself violently again*). O, how close it is! Air—give me air! Open the window.

TRIS. Why, I just closed it, at your command. (*Stands with hands spread out in comical dismay.*)

LADY H. (*impatiently*). Open it, open it—don't you hear? Quick, air! (*very affectedly*).

(TRIS. *runs, trottingly, to open the window.*)

NAN. (*aside*). My lord is running for the prize.

(*Here the song of the servants bound for Richmond fair is heard outside.*)

NO. 3a.

CHO. (*singing*). Hither come, linger not,
Fate a home shall allot;
She who works and not shirks,
Finds her fun, when 'tis done.

LADY H. Hear them sing!

CHO. Hither come, take your pick,
We will serve through thin and thick,
Masters kind, come and bind,
If we find you to our mind.

NAN. It's quite amusing!

TRIS. Nonsense! you must be mad.

NAN. You do not find them funny?

TRIS. Servants ignorant and bad.

LADY H. Ah, but they are gay and happy!

NAN. O, the bound girls, I now remember!
This is Richmond market day.
Where the servants, flocking yearly,
Seek new masters, better pay.

TRIS. Stupid custom!

NAN. But 'tis an old one.

LADY H. (*goes to window*). I might join them.
What a thought!
How I'd like to go among them,
See such curious prizes bought!

TRIS. What a notion! What folly's this?

LADY H. Nancy, get the peasant costumes ready
That we wore at the fancy dress ball.

(NANCY *is busy at chiffonier at one side. Tosses bright colored kerchief out.* LADY H. *picks it up and throws it over her head as the singing goes on.*)

TRIS. You'd degrade yourself like this?

LADY H. Just amuse myself, that's all.
Hurry Nancy, we must run,
Now at last I'll have some fun!
Martha (*curtseys*), Nancy (*curtseys*) and—old John!

(*Tosses her kerchief over* TRISTAN'S *head, blinding him.* TRIS. *is bewildered, kerchief hanging over one eye.*)

TRIS. Who is John? What old John?

LADY H. Who but you?You are old John!

TRIS. I? I old John?No that's too much.

(*Snatches off kerchief and throws it down.*)

LADY H. Sir Tristan, whene'er the fair we woo, sir,
With caprices we comply,
Else we see tears fall in showers,
See, dear John, these charming flowers—

(*Gives him flowers from his own nosegay. He kisses her hand, puts flowers in coat.*)

LADY H. Take them, nor my prayer deny!
(*lifts skirt at side and dances a step*).
With the village people dancing,
Nancy's partner you're enroll'd.

TRIS. No, in sooth I'm far too old.

LADY H. Stuff! In spite of years advancing,
Man can do all, if he's bold.

NAN. (*drags him about stage dancing*).
This way, that way, loosely hopping,
Each one jigging as he can,
Lumb'ring, stumbling, never stopping,
Mighty maze without a plan.

TRIS. Then, I must—

LADY H. I command it!

TRIS. But no, I can't.

LADY H. Your paces show!

TRIS. But my rank,—

NAN. How well you stand it!
That's well I vow.

(*They all dance and the ladies sing la-la-la.*)

LADY H. Danced superbly!

NAN. What a figure.

TRIS. I shall soon be out of breath.

NAN. Come, more vigor! come, more vigor!

TRIS. This I'm sure will be my death.

LADY H. AND NAN. Come, old John, come, old John,
'Tis we who ask, so come along.

TRIS. This is too much! I, old John? What I?

(*All run off stage dancing,* TRISTAN *between the two ladies, who drag him.*)

Curtain.

ACT TWO.

(Curtain rises on Richmond market place. Stall around sides of stage and back. In foreground, tables and benches; side show of some funny sort. Tents at one side. Country folk walking about, farmers and wives.)

NO. 4.

CHO. Come, O maidens fair,
Yes, come, but come with cheerful looks!
Handsome is as handsome does,
The rule that suits our books.
Hasten, hasten, cheerful maidens,
Do not linger on the way,
Soon the Hiring Fair will open
And advancing is the day.
Done! once the bargain is agreed to
Neither can undo it.
Done! faithful servants, kindly masters,
Neither then will rue it.
Neatness is the best of graces,
Smooth of hair come every one;
In a row all take your places,
Soon the choosing will be done.
If you'll be but quick and neat
And try to do your best,
You will find a happy home,
And the pay of your deserving. Come!
Find a home, yes, come.

(Enter serving maids, arm in arm. Farmers go to meet them.)

SERVANTS' CHO. Hither come, linger not,
Fate a home will allot, etc.

FARMERS AND WIVES. Come this way, don't delay, We have waited you many a day.

SERV. Oh, not now, but tomorrow,
We are tired, we are shy.

FARMERS. Handsome is that handsome does,
The best rule that ever was.

(*Farmers and wives try to bring servants into a line forward on stage. The servants hold back.*)

SERV. Since the day how we have run,
Now we shall know,
Just where each girl is going to go.
Now our journey's o'er and here we rest with you at last,
After many a mile so long and lone is over past.

(*Servants scatter about stage, some lying down as if to rest, as* LIONEL *and* PLUNKET *enter. They come on talking.* PLUNKET *is dressed as a peasant farmer and carries a whip. Lionel is dressed as a gentleman, but plainly.*)

PLUNKET. Here is a jolly howdoyoudo. What a clatter they make! The farmers are all going to engage servants for the coming year out of this crowd of chattering hussies. It is a good thing to take your time to choose, though, for once the bargain is made you have to stick to it for at least a year. What do you say, Lionel? Have you picked out your Betsy Ann?

LIONEL. Betsy Ann—what do you mean? (*He speaks absently, slowly, and his demeanor throughout is one of dreamy abstraction. He is very grave and pensive, altogether a young man who would be likely to take a love affair very seriously and perhaps lose his mental balance temporarily over it.*)

PLUN. I mean our serving girl. You know mother put it in her will that we must keep up the farm together. So now like two good housewives we must fly around and choose a maid. Her name may be Sally or Katy or Jane, but I shall call her Betsy Ann! (*Laughs.*)

LIO. I shall always remember your dear mother and be grateful.

PLUN. Yes, she was a good woman and a good mother, aye, a good manager, too. She knew how to make the maids attend to their work.

LIO. But she was kind. She was always so kind to me.

PLUN. Yes, she loved you. If you had been her own child she could not have tended you more anxiously. You were a mere baby when your father died and left you in our care. No one could help trying to make up your loss to you, somehow. If I'd a mind I might have been jealous of you. I was always the one who got the scoldings. I suppose mother owed them to me, for I was her own naughty boy!

LIO. You have always been a real brother to me, Plunket. No helpless child could have had a happier fate than to find home with you.

PLUN. You had no one but mother and me, old chap, don't you see? What else could a fellow do but try to keep you heartened up a little? (*Laughs with some embarrassment.*)

LIO. And yet even now we do not know who I really am. We shall never know, unless some day my father's ring (*lifts his hand*) may serve to clear up the mystery at last. (*Sings.*)

NO. 5.

LIO. O'er my life from boyhood tender,
You have watched with sheltering care,
You your all would fain surrender,
With the orphan child to share.
You fulfilled a father's duty,
When he left me to your love,
Ah, he heard my mother calling,
Heard her call from heaven above.

PLUN. Nor his rank nor name he told us,
Nor the secret dar'd unseal (*touches* LIONEL'S *hand*),
This his ring one day shall tell it,
All the mystery yet reveal.
On your finger when he placed it,"
This may change his fate," he sighed,
"This my ring the Queen will honor
Should misfortune e'er betide."

LIO. Brother mine, 'mid courtly splendors
My vain longings ne'er shall rove,
Ah, no light on earth allures me,
Save the tender glow of love.
No strange joys I'd earn for yonder,
Peace and sweet content are here,'
Mid the fields are simple pleasures,
Calm affection, tried and dear.

(*A bell from the village church gives the signal for the fair to begin. Sheriff enters pompously, the farmers and wives and servants flock after him. He is dressed in wig, hat and robe. He has a staff of office. A girl is pushed against him in the crowd. He waves her back majestically, at arm's length and speaks.*)

SHERIFF (*speaks*) Let the rabble stand back. Room for the majesty of the law. Ahem!

GIRL (*speaks pertly*). My, ain't he the big wig, though! (*Tweaks at his wig from behind and pulls it partly off. His hat falls off. She picks it up and runs.*)

SHERIFF. Ouch! (*Grabs at wig with one hand and runs after the girl, shaking his staff at her. Another girl gets in his way; they dodge back and forth, till she puts her two hands, one each side of his face and tries to kiss him.*)

GIRL (*speaks*). There, there, old gentleman, don't feel so bad over a bit of our fun!

> (SHERIFF *ducks to avoid kiss and leaves wig in her hands. He runs wildly about stage, clutching alternately at his bald head, and at the wig, which the girls toss back and forth, while he tries to snatch it. Finally one of the farmers catches it and restores it to sheriff. He puts it on and some one brings him his hat.*)

FARMER (*speaks*). Young hussies, you must do better than this when you get to working for us. Behave yourselves, now!

SHERIFF (*much distressed, almost weeping with rage*). I bind you all over to keep the peace on penalty of 10 shillings fine. (*Pounds with his staff.*) Does the majesty of the law mean naught to ye? Silence (*they laugh*), you low bred populace. But what can one expect from populace? Pah! They are beneath my notice. (*Looks scornfully at them while music begins. A girl laughingly sticks out her tongue at him. He glares at her. She does it again. He looks hastily away and then back. She throws him a kiss, and all the rest follow suit. He scowls, but his face gradually softens into a smirk. The farmers drag the girls back into a line. Sheriff unrolls a parchment, that he takes from pocket of his big gown. He sings.*)

NO. 6.

SHERIFF. We, Anne, Queen of England, greet ye!
(*Snatches off his hat, farmers do the same.*)
Bonnets off, and mine likewise.
I no ceremony spare!
We hereby do recognize
Ev'ry contract good and sound
Made in Richmond market bound;
Every lass who here is hired,
Dating from this very day,
Till the year is full expired,
Must with her new master stay.

If he pay the money down
The bargain cannot be undone.
Have you heard?

CHO. We know, sir, it is so, sir.

SHER. Now you stand up in a row.

(*Servants stand in line; he arranges them.*)

Tell us, Moll, what you can do.

(*One maid steps forward a little, bobs a curtsey.*)

1ST MAID. I can darn, sir, I can sew, sir,
I can milk and I can mow, sir.
I can bake and mend and make
And garden beds I can weed and rake.

1ST FARMER (*steps forward*). All for just four pounds a year. Well, at that she is not dear. (*Takes girl one side.*)

SHER. (*to next girl*). Now, my lass, what can you do?

2D MAID. (*curtseys*). I can mend, sir, sew a button,
On old socks new feet can put on,
I can roast and boil and stew,
Can churn and chop and also brew.

SHER. Five pounds a year,
'Tis for a song, now!

2D FARMER (*steps up and leads her aside*).
Here's my hand, done! Come along!

Sher. Come, it's your turn now to speak.

3D MAID. (*curtseys*). I can clean, sir, I can scrub, sir,
I'm a good one at a tub, sir,Yes, to every sort of work,
My hand I turn and never shirk.

SHER. Kitty Bell and Johnny Snell,
And Nelly Browne and Sally Towne.

CHO. OF SERVANTS. How to care for babes I know, sir,
Bless 'em, I do love 'em so, sir,
I can take the cows to graze, sir,
And of poultry know the ways, sir;
I can bake and boil and brew, sir,
I can sew on buttons, too.

MEN. I'm accustomed pigs to keep, sir,
Also, horses, cows and sheep, sir,
Pork and beef in brine I steep, sir,
Yes, and do the mowing cheap, sir;
I can dig a garden bed
And make a cabbage grow a head.
Ha, if you pay the cash,
We'll work just like a flash.
Ho, it's very clear,
All settled for a year.
Ho, now the deed is done,
We'll work like fun!

(*The servants flock around him as they sing and gather closer and closer till he puts his hands over his ears and tries to get away from them. They crowd around and sing into his face and over his shoulders.*)

SHER. *(with hands at ears*). Stop your cackling! You'll make me deaf!

FARMERS. We are ready to choose, but one at a time, please.

(*Girls drop back into line; farmers move about among them,* LIONEL *and* PLUNKET *also, as if bargaining with them. Enter* LADY HARRIET, NANCY *and* TRISTAN *in peasant costume.*)

LADY H. Come on, John! Courage man! Nobody's going to hurt you!

NAN. Come, friend John! Don't look so scared. We'll take care of you!

TRIS. John? O, im-pos-si-ble! O, pre-pos-ter-ous! I don't like this one bit. It is most unseemly. Yet—where beauty leads, love fain must follow.

LADY H. How gay they all seem! They at least are happy.

TRIS. I know I am not! I never felt less jolly before (*plaintively*) in all my life. (*Aside.*) I feel as if I were going to cry. (*Face works.*)

(PLUNKET *and* LIONEL *approach the three and stand at a short distance, gazing at* LADY H. *and* NANCY.)

PLUN. Jove! There's a brace of darlings!

LIO. Yes, they are very pretty girls.

PLUN. Rather slim built for hard work, though.

LIO. They might do house work?

PLUN. Yes, they might serve indoors. I don't know—(*pauses*)

TRIS. See those clodhoppers! How they stare at you. O, do be persuaded to leave this horrid, horrid place.

LADY H. *and* NAN (*together*). No, indeed. We like it and we are going to stay.

TRIS. I think those fellows are very suspicious looking characters. A pair of rogues. Let's go (*urging them by taking their arms*).

LADY H. I'm not under your orders, sir. It is my pleasure to stay. I'll do exactly as I choose!

TRIS. Well, I wash my hands of all responsibility. Don't say I didn't warn you.

NAN (*sees that* PLUNKET *and* LIONEL *are watching her*). Those lads have an eye for a good thing, though. (*To* TRISTAN.) We'll take all the blame. No one shall say that you led us into mischief, poor dear!

LADY H. Yes, cousin, you are exonerated. Whatever happens, be it upon my own rash head. But I will not go! (*Emphatically.*)

PLUN. (*overhears last words*). You hear, sir? She will not go with you. Don't annoy the girls any further. (*To girls.*) Call on us if he bothers you. (*To* TRIS., *who looks daggers.*) But cheer up! There are plenty more maids yonder. Hi, girls (*turns to the servants*). Here's a chap wants a good maid, and he looks as if he could pay well, too.

TRIS. Oh! what a beastly joke! He's taking liberties with me! (*He looks scared and affronted.*)

(LADY H. *and* NANCY *laugh together over* TRISTAN'S *plight as the girls come forward and surround him.*)

ALL (*chattering*). I can mow, I can sew, I can reap, I can sweep, I can bake and make, I can boil and stew, I can churn and brew! (*All speak different lines from the part just sung and make a great clatter and confusion.* TRISTAN *dodges among them and runs off, the girls following him.*)

LADY H. He has taken refuge in flight!

NAN. Let's hope he won't forget us.

LADY H. (*nervously*). See those men. They are still looking at us.

NAN. They seem to have taken a fancy to us, that's plain.

PLUN. (*to* LIONEL). One of them would be just what we want, I think—the younger one, now. (*Nods at* NANCY.)

LIONEL. It would never do to separate them. See how shy they are.

LADY H. (*to* NANCY). That one seems quite bashful, doesn't he? I wonder how such peasants talk?

NAN. Bad grammar, for one thing.

PLUN. (*to* LIONEL). What are you afraid of? Go speak to them.

LIO. I'm afraid to.

PLUN. Silly noodle! Just watch me. (*Advances boldly as if to speak to the ladies, stops suddenly and goes back.*)

NAN. The big one is dumb, too; aren't they stupid! Let's go.

LADY H. (*turns to follow* TRISTAN). I suppose we'd better—

(*Hesitates and looks back at the two men.*)

PLUN. We must not let such a chance slip. Servant girls like those are not found every day. I have taken a fancy to that big one and I don't mean to let her get away. Courage, Plunket! (*He advances again, again hesitates, and snapping his fingers at himself, advances and speaks.*) Wait a moment, girls! We've decided we like you. If you're as smart as you look you can have a good place with us for years.

LIO. Yes, for years and years!

LADY H. You mean as your servants?

PLUN. Of course! What else?

NAN. (*laughing*). Ha! ha! ha! what a joke!

LIO. What is there to laugh at?

PLUN. So long as they do their work, the more they laugh, the better.

LADY H. *and* NAN. Work! We!

PLUN. (*to* NAN.). I'll give you the care of the geese and pigs and chickens. (*To* LADY H.) You shall have charge of the garden—weed it, and gather potatoes and corn.

LIO. O come! that's too hard for her. Let her do housework—

PLUN. And darn our socks and mend our shirts? Very well. We'll pay you fifty crowns a year. For extras there'll be a pint of ale on Sundays and plum pudding on New Years.

LADY H. Who could refuse such a tempting offer? (*Laughs.*)

NAN. Now I know what I am worth, at last! (*Laughs.*)

PLUN. *and* LIO. (*eagerly*). You agree?

LADY H. *and* NAN. Yes! yes! We agree! (*They shake hands.*)

PLUN. It's a bargain! Here's the money down!

(LADY H. *and* NAN. *each put the money in their purse, laughing together.*)

NO. 7.

LADY H. *and* NAN. (*sing*).
See what grace they show in mien and bearing,
Of our sport, I'm bound, I say, to see the end;
Money's paid and we must keep our bargain,
Men so courteous never will offend.

LIO. *and* PLUN.
Two young maids so well set up and charming,
Ne'er was city girl that equalled these of mine;
They are jewels, pretty, kind and cheerful,
Faith, I'll tell them so, and lose no time.

(*At close of quartette* TRISTAN *comes back to stage, evidently exhausted and much dishevelled; the servants follow him and again surround him.*)

TRIS. Oh, I thought I had eluded them! Leave off! Here's money! (*Throws a purse.*) Plague on your crazy pack! (*The girls run to divide the money.*) Ho! what is this? (*He advances toward* PLUNKET, *who has hold of* NANCY'S *arm.*) You forget yourself! Forbear!

PLUN. Who are you? What do you want? (*A tussel threatens between the two men.* TRISTAN *backs down, afraid.*)

LADY H. There, there! it's all right! (*To* TRISTAN.) We are ready to go now. (*Takes his arm.*)

PLUN. I'd like to see you! With my money in your purse! You stay with us!

TRIS. Fellow! do you know who this is?

LADY H. (*aside to* TRIS.) No! no! don't betray me! Think what a scandal if this got to court! Don't you dare to tell them who I am!

NAN. (*aside*). We should be disgraced forever. Rather die than that!

TRIS. Well, come, then. It is time for me to insist. I require you to come with me. (*Tries to lead them off.*)

PLUN. (*interferes*). Not so fast! You belong here. These are my maids, hired and cash paid in advance! Ask the sheriff!

SHERIFF (*who has approached during the altercation, after a long confab with one of the other girls at one side*). Have you taken the money?

LADY H. (*draws it out of her purse and flings it at* LIONEL). Yes. But there it is; I had forgotten it.

(LIONEL *picks it up and offers it back. She refuses it. He insists.*)

SHERIFF. You took it of your own free will and now it is a bargain. You are bound to serve for one year. Highty, tighty! Do you think you can play fast and loose with a master in that fashion? No, no! Bound you are to him and with him you must go!

(*During final chorus* PLUN. *drives up his horse and cart and the two girls are handed into the cart. They drive away.* TRISTAN *tries to follow, but is restrained by the crowd. If the horse and cart cannot be had, the two girls may dodge about among the crowd, the men following them, and run off at last, the men chasing them.*)

NO. 7a.FINALE.

CHORUS.Now our journey's o'er and here we rest with you at last,
After many a mile so long and lone is over past.

(*Curtain.*)

ACT THREE.

(The third act opens in the great hall of the farmhouse of LIONEL *and* PLUNKET. *At one side of stage at back is an outside door; on the other side, a window with bench in front of it. Another door is on the left. There are several chairs. A flight of stairs goes up from the right side, back corner. Two spinning wheels stand at rear, and farm tools hang about the walls.*

During the instrumental prelude the outside door opens and the two men, LIONEL *and* PLUNKET, *enter, inviting the girls,* LADY H. *and* NANCY, *who are behind, to come in. They come in slowly, hesitatingly, half afraid.)*

NO. 8.

PLUN. *and* LIO. (*sing*).Come in, my pretty maidens,
We've reached our home, you see.

LADY H. *and* NAN. O, we are in a pretty fix,
We only long to flee.
How safely to escape them
We'll seek from morn till mirk.

(*Girls sit down*). O, what a shabby dwelling,
O, how they'll make us work.

LIO. *and* PLUN. Now, look alive!
Of work don't be afraid.

LADY H. *and* NAN. There's no hope, I'm afraid.
We've come to the end of our jest at last.

NO. 9.

PLUN. (*points to door at left*).
That's the room I mean to give them.

LADY H. *and* NAN. (*rising*).
Then good night, then good night.
(*Starting toward door.*)

PLUN. What's that you say?
First put everything aright.

LADY H. O, with cold I'm all a-shiver!

NAN. O, I quake in every member.

LIO. Both to fainting, seem inclined.

PLUN. Why, to spoil them you've a mind.

NAN. This denouement is provoking.

PLUN. You've not told us your names yet, my maids.

LADY H. *and* NAN. We!

LIO. Yes, obey!

PLUN. Obey at once, no joking.

LADY H. Martha is my name.

LIO. Martha?

LADY H. (*looks at him*). Yes.

PLUN. Now, tell yours.

NAN. (*aside*). Mad masquerading!

PLUN. Don't you know it?

NAN. Betsy Ann!

PLUN. Betsy Ann? I rather like it!
Come here, my girl: lend a hand then, will you, Betsy?
(*Pulls off his coat and offers it to her.*)
Take my coat and hang it up.

NAN. Do't yourself!

PLUN. You lazy hussy!

LIO. Come, you frighten her by scolding.
Speak more gently, say like that—
Martha, take away my hat.

(*Holds it toward her.* MARTHA *stamps her foot, slaps hat out of his hand and walks up stage. He, bewildered, hangs up his own hat.*)

LIO. O, how have I offended?
I cannot understand.
Yes, I'm awfully perplexed.
Why should she act so grand?

PLUN. Ah, what can be the matter?
I do not understand.
Some secret she is screening,
Her manner is so grand.

NAN. Ah, on my dignity I stand.
They give an order quite off hand!

LADY H. To tyranny I'll ne'er give in,
We'll fight them now, to win.
He thinks me strange and haughty
But on my right I stand,
Commanding I must withstand him,
Resist his harsh demand.

NO. 10.

PLUN. (*draws spinning wheels to center of stage*).
Come, your task awaits, the whirring wheel and spindle!

LADY H. *and* NAN. Set us spinning? We're to spin?

LIO. Yes, of course.

PLUN. So begin.
How your claims to skill do dwindle.

LADY H. and NAN. Ha, ha, ha, spin, sir?

PLUN. (*imitating her laughter in anger*).
Ha, ha, ha, so set to work and spin your task!
What you here for, may I ask?
Just to hold your hands and chatter?
What's the matter?

NAN. What a clatter.

LIO. Pray be calm, now, they're afraid.

PLUN. Peace! Come, spin! we won't be cheated.

LADY H. *and* NAN. How, sir?

LIO. What?

PLUN. Come, come.(*Places chairs at spinning wheels.*)

PLUN. Be seated. (*They sit.*)

LADY H. *and* NAN. 'Tis done.

PLUN. Good! Now then, proceed.
(*Imitating sound of spinning wheel.*)
Thrum, thrum, thrum.

NAN. I can't, indeed.

LIO. Here's the distaff, firmly grasp it (*To* LADY H.),'Twixt your fingers seize the skein.

LADY H. Must we with wet fingers clasp it?
Turn it? No, I won't!
How so? In vain.
I cannot, I cannot.
Place yourself then at the wheel.

(*The two girls rise and the men sit one at each wheel.*)

PLUN. We'll make it reel.

ALL. While the wheel is swiftly spinning
Round it thus the flax is roll'd,
But moistened just at the beginning,
That more firmly it may hold.
See the wheel so swiftly spinning,
To thread the flax is thinning.

(NANCY *suddenly throws* PLUNKET'S *wheel over and runs off stage by back door*, PLUNKET *after her.*)

(LADY H. *turns to follow* NANCY. *Speaks.*)

LADY H. Nan—Betsy Ann! O stay with me! Heavens, she's left me!

LIO. Martha, why are you going? Are you afraid to stay alone with me?

LADY H. Afraid? Of you? Oh, no. (*Smiles, but still hesitates.*)

LIO. (*aside*). How could I ever have spoken harshly to her?

LADY H. (*aside*). Where *has* Nancy gone?

LIO. Martha, I will never again ask any toil of you, or any service that you dislike. Martha, I never saw any one before that seemed to me so pretty and so sweet! Are all girls as lovely as you?

LADY H. Don't you know?

LIO. I never noticed a girl before.

LADY H. (*archly*). Where have your eyes been?

LIO. Dreaming, I guess. I feel as if I had just awakened to all the beauty and joy there is in the world!

LADY H. Alas! and I feel as if I have already learned how shallow are all earthly joys! (*Pensively.*)

LIO. Poor little maid! You have had too hard a life. Such service has burdened you with care too soon. Here you will never again have to labor beyond your strength. I would myself do all disagreeable tasks rather than require them of you.

LADY H. Oh, I am a good-for-nothing. I never did a real day's work in all my life.

LIO. You must not scold yourself. Martha is my servant now, and I would not exchange her for a dozen others.

LADY H. But can you not see that I am not worth my salt? I shall only be an expense to you. I cannot earn a shilling a week. See my hands. (*Shows them.*) Do they look like useful members?

LIO. (*takes them in his hands*). So white and soft! Surely never servant before had such pretty fingers. Not a spot of toil!

LADY H. And so of course they are of no use to you, and you will not keep me here any longer. You will let them go—this useless pair of hands?

LIO. I cannot let them go!

LADY H. (*tries to withdraw her hands*). But if I work they will become hard and stained. I have never been taught—

LIO. Never worked before? Then I will teach you and share your every task. What *can* you do?

LADY H. I can sing a little.

LIO And you can smile. (*He looks at her; her eyes fall.*)

LADY H. Sing and smile! A working maid must do something more than that.

LIO. If you will stay with me here and smile and sing, you shall see how pleasant you will find it. You shall have no rough tasks. You shall have only kindness and happiness. You shall be like a sister in this house. These little hands will dispense blessing and peace. (*Kisses them.*)

LADY H. (*draws her hands away and walks to the door. He follows.*) Is it thus that masters treat a servant? (*With dignity.*)

LIO. Forgive me! I have forgotten everything. O, would that your station were different—or mine!

LADY H. (*turns back*). My station?—(*recollects herself*). But I am only a serving lass! (*She laughs and returns down stage.*)

LIO. And so you must do what I bid you. I require of you a song.

LADY H. Oh, I am too shy to sing.

LIO. (*takes the flowers from her dress*). I'll exchange this nosegay for a song. (*Music of "Last Rose of Summer" may be played softly here.*)

LADY H. Ah! you jest.

LIO. No, I command!

LADY H. (*coldly*). Command, sir?

LIO. Nay, I entreat (*kneels, laughingly*).

(LADY H. *takes one of the flowers he offers, and plays with it as she sings. He puts the other flowers presently into the breast of his coat.*)

LADY H. Ah, your entreaty I cannot withstand. (*Sings.*)

NO. 11.

LADY H. (*sings*). 'Tis the last rose of summer,
blooming alone;
All her lovely companions
Are faded and gone.
No flower of her kindred,
No rosebud is nigh,
To reflect back her blushes
Or give sigh for sigh.
I'll not leave thee, thou lone one,
To pine on the stem,
Since the lovely are faded,
Go sleep thou with them.
Thus kindly I'll scatter
Thy leaves o'er the bed,
Where thy mates of the garden
Lie scentless and dead.

(*Aside.*) His eyes betray he loves me,
Spite my lowly seeming lot,
My rank I must remember,
Ah, would 'twere all forgot.
His heart is true and loyal,
Tie me her loves alone,
O, would I were the lowly maid
He longs to make his own.

LIO. All my proud rank forgetting
For the maid I love alone,
I'd lift her from her low estate,
And make her all my own.

LIO. (*speaks*). Martha!

LADY H. Master!

LIO. My heart can no longer be denied. I have loved you from the first moment I saw you yonder at Richmond market. Martha (*takes her hand again*).

LADY H. Ah, no, no! (*Turns her face away.*)

LIO. Love at first sight! First love at first sight!

LADY H. No more, no more! Oh, be silent!

LIO. Martha, I shall never love woman but you. (*Puts his arm around her.*)

LADY H. (*tries to escape*). Oh, I must go, I must go! (*Pulls away.*)

LIO. Stay and hear me. Stay—and be my wife!—

LADY H. Oh, what is he saying?

LIO. See, I am at your feet—in earnest now! (*Kneels.*)

LADY H. (*aside*). Oh, how can I elude him? (*Begins to laugh.*) Don't think me heartless, but really (*affectedly*) to see you kneeling there is so funny!

LIO. But when we are married all difference of birth and station will be wiped out; you will forget that you were once my servant; you will have in me forever a slave!

LADY H. (*is touched, and then begins to laugh hysterically again*). Ha! ha! ha! This is ridiculous! If you only knew how funny you are!

(PLUNKET *runs on dragging* NANCY. LIONEL *rises and* LADY H. *runs toward* NANCY *whom* PLUNKET *swings on to the stage.*)

PLUN. There, my girl! Don't you try that game again! Where do you suppose she was? the vixen! In the kitchen, smashing dishes, bottles, glasses, everything she could lay her hands on! She made me look lively, too, before I caught her. My eye!

NAN. If you don't let me go, I'll scratch it out!

PLUN. (*releasing her*). Jupiter! I believe you would! She has spirit. I confess I like to see it.

NAN. Martha, Martha, what are we going to do? (*Twelve o'clock strikes slowly as they speak.*)

PLUN. Pooh! What ails you now? My patience is worn out! Get to bed, you idle baggage! You are a hard case, that's easy to see.

(*Quartet follows.*)

LADY H., NAN., PLUN. *and* LIO. Midnight chimes sound afar!

LIO. If the maid her love refuse me,
Yet I pledge my faithful heart,
In her glance faint hope is smiling,
Bringing comfort ere here we part.

NAN. Of our foolish prank I'm weary,
Tho' in play 'twas fain begun;
Yet our childish trick is working
Pain and sorrow to every one.So good night!

PLUN. Now good night and sleep in quiet,
Tho' you're fractious I am kind,
Naughty girls to work must settle,
Learn to mind.

LADY H. That to wound his heart I'm fated
Fills my heart with pity and pain,
Ah, our mad caprice is working
Pain and sorrow, all in vain.

LIO. Though her love she refuse me,
Yet I pledge my faithful heart,
So good night, good night!

(Girls go out and close door, before orchestral ending. Then the men retire after locking the outer door. Girls open their door again, peep out, run back, and shut door, etc.; then come out again, watching with finger on lips for interruptions. They speak.)

LADY H. Nancy!

NANCY. My lady.

LADY H. This is our chance.

NANCY. What shall we do?

LADY H. What do *you* say?

NAN. Can we escape so—all alone?

LADY H. We are locked in, besides.

NAN. What an awful time we are having!

LADY H. Awful day—aw-ful-ler night—the day was bad, but this is worse. We *are* in a scrape!

NAN, Still—those fellows might be worse! (*Looks at* LADY H. *slyly.*)

LADY H. (*with dignity*). They are well meaning.

NAN. (*archly*). And polite.

LADY H. If the Queen should hear of it!

NAN. Good bye us!

(*A noise is heard outside at window.*)

LADY H. (*grasps* NANCY *and they run across stage to their door*). What is it? O who is coming?

NAN. Steps—a voice—help is near!

TRISTAN (*outside whispers loudly*). Cousin, cousin!

LADY H. Tristan! O joy! O horrors!

NAN. What will he think?

LADY H. He will scold us—and we deserve it. But he will save us!

(TRISTAN *enters through the window which girls help him open.*)

TRIS. Yes, here I am, faithful still. Cousin. (*Looks around.*) What a vulgar habitation! That I should live to see you in a place like this. (*Shudders.*)

NAN. Hush! You'll wake everybody up.

LADY H. Don't stop to preach. Just go.

TRIS. I have a carriage at the corner. Come, make haste.

(*They tiptoe about and sing.*)

NO. 12.

LADY H. *and* NAN. Hasten then, to fortune trust our lot,
thee well, thou humble cot.
'Tis our only chance to fly,

We'll not stop to say good bye.

TRIS. Let's be off now in a hurry,
For their anger we'll not worry,

'Tis your only chance to fly,
We'll not stop to say good bye.

(As the curtain falls they have all three climbed out of window.)

Curtain.

ACT FOUR.

(*A forest. A small inn at left.* PLUNKET *and several of his farm hands discovered sitting at table.* PLUNKET *rises and sings his song, the men joining in chorus.*)

NO. 13.

PLUN. Come, can you tell me, read me the riddle,
What to our lordly British name
Gives power and fame—Come, say?
Ha, 'tis old porter, brown and stout,
None that is like it round about,
The Briton's pride, he'll aye confide,
In porter's power, whatever betide.

Yes, hurrah, hurrah for old English ale,
The friend in need who can never fail,
Hurrah,—tra, la, la, la, la, la!

Listen my lads and tell me truly
What in our land you most do prize?
What's worth your eyes? Come, say?
Ho! 'tis your nut-brown foaming beer,
See how it heaps the beaker here—
The Briton's pride, he'll aye confide, in porter's power, whatever betide.

CHO. Yes, hurrah! hurrah for the old English ale, etc.

(*At close of chorus after* PLUNKET'S *song, horns are heard outside,—the opening strains of the next number. When it stops, at end of second brace, he speaks.*)

PLUN. Aha! the hunt is up. They told me the Queen would hunt today.

ONE OF MEN. Yes, with all her ladies. No doubt the men-folk will follow, too!

PLUN. Start along, you, then. I'll go in and pay the score.

(*Men leave stage,* PLUNKET *enters the inn.*)

(*As music begins again the court ladies run on in hunting costume. They wear short walking skirts, caps and high boots, perhaps, and all carry long spears.* NANCY *is with them. She carries a whip instead of a spear, and wears a long riding habit draped up over high boots.*)

No. 14.

CHORUS. All we ladies of the court
Are lovers of sport of every sort;
Every hunting cry we know,
As hark tally ho, view tally ho!
We can handle dart and bow,
O yes, we can dart after a beau;
We can shoot and ride and row,
Can play at ball, dance at them all;
With rings and things we prancing go,
Ho ho! and tally ho! we know,
And how to catch a beau!

(*Girls stroll about stage and sit at table.* NANCY *comes forward alone.*)

No. 15.

NAN. (*sings*). Gay of heart, I have not known how to weep,
How to be sorry and wan;
Vigil to keep.
Yet alas, sighs are my portion and pain,
Tears that flow ever in vain,
Hindering sleep.
There's a voice speaks in my heart night and day,
What is the word soft it would say?
Ah, voice of love so true and deep,
Ah, soul of faith my answer keep.
Memory still calls one face to my heart,
O light of my life forever thou art;
O voice of love so true and deep,
Face so dear, light of my heart
Forever thou art.

(*She turns to the others who gather round her.*)

NAN. Hunters fair, now beware,
Lest you fall into a snare.
Haste away, don't delay,
Lest you lose your pretty prey.
Love's a sprite soon takes flight,
Chance and change are his delight;
Use your eyes, win the prize,
Ere too soon he flies.

Love's a hunter, too, they say,
Draws his bow, alackaday!
Hit, we're fain to bear the pain,
Flight is vain.

CHORUS. Yes, Cupid blind,
Thy darts are swifter far than wind.

(*At end of chorus* PLUNKET *re-enters from the inn.*)

PLUNKET. Halloo! There seems to be good game afoot here. I'll see if I have any luck at the chase myself! (*Walks towards the ladies.*)

NAN. (*looking around*). Where can Lady Harriet be? She seems to avoid society more than ever. She is very unhappy, and has been so ever since—(*addresses* PLUNKET) My good man, can you tell me—(*stops in agitation*)

PLUN. What, Betsy Ann! You? In these togs!

NAN. (*distantly*). Well, my good man, what is it?

PLUN. I am not your good man! But you are my bad maid! Just you wait! I'll make you pay for all the trouble you've given me. What are you doing here in this masquerade?

NAN. Are you crazy?

PLUN. No use to pretend! I know you. Come along home with me!

NAN. (*shrieks as he seizes her wrist*). Help! Help!

PLUN. What a wicked little hussy you are!

NAN. What an impudent big clodhopper you are!

(*The ladies turn back towards* NANCY.)

NAN. Here is game for you, girls. Let's see how he will like your spears!

(*Ladies surround* PLUNKET *and threaten him.*)

CHORUS (*speaking all together*). We'll give him a taste of our spear points! He won't bother her long! At him, now! There's safety in numbers! (*Repeating.*)

PLUN. Gently, gently—Hold on! This is turning the tables in good earnest. Ouch!!! Those remarks are a little too pointed for me. (*Dodges.*) I never expected to see myself run from a woman, but here goes! (*He runs off, the ladies after him, shouting incoherently, as above.*NANCY *enters inn.*)

(*Enter* LIONEL. *He looks more absent-minded and dreamy than ever. He seems dejected and ill. Murmurs to himself.*)

LIO. I will detach thee from thy frail trembling stem. O thou lovely rose of summer, thou shalt lie upon my heart, forever more! (*Takes withered flower from his breast and kisses it, then looks around him.*)

Where am I? I feel that I am near her. Martha, Martha! thou star of my heart! I see her before me, with her beautiful pure smile, radiant in youth and sweetness. O Martha, I feel thee near! (*Sings.*)

NO. 16.

LIO. O, when she rose fair on my sight,
Radiant, lovely, like dawning light,
Flow'd all my heart forth to her own,
Tribute to beauty bright.
Joy reviv'd and my thought
Sang like woodlands after rain,
Hope for me shone again,
Lighting all my hours of pain.
Gladness made all my heart
Bright as meadows pearl'd with dew,
For I dream'd love's sweet dream
Ever old, yet young like dawn
And ever new!

O, when she rose, fair on my sight, etc.
Martha, Martha, must I lose thee,
Life has naught can peace restore!
Thou, my comfort, peace and pleasure,
Reft of thy sweet looks I die!

(*At the close of his song* LIONEL *goes to the back of stage and stands alone.* SIR TRISTAN *and* LADY HARRIET *enter.*)

TRIS. The ladies are all out of sight. Why did you leave their company, fair cousin?

LADY H. (*pointedly*). Because I wished to be alone!

TRISTAN. To remain alone—with me?

LADY H. With you?—(*laughs a little*) Alone or with you—it's quite the same thing!—I am low-spirited, that is what I mean. I don't want to see anybody.

TRIS. What should make you so sad?

LADY H. I am sure I know no more than you about it. It is a mystery even to myself.

TRIS. But to remain alone in this secluded spot—is it quite—er—you know—

LADY H. But it is exactly what I want. Good bye!

TRIS. But I will soon return—soon—soon—(*looks back anxiously as he goes*)

LADY H. Oh, it is so good to be alone, with only my sad memories for company! But if *he* were only here—this loneliness were sweet.

LIO. (*wanders down stage and sees her*). Ah! that voice!

LADY H. Oh, heaven—what do I see?—

LIONEL. A lady?—

LADY H. He is here, then—even as I said!

LIO. 'Tis she—even as I said—Martha, Martha!

LADY H. O, what shall I do now? How shall I elude him?—

LIO. O, Martha, you have come back to me—O, thank heaven, thank heaven! It is Martha, her very self—Martha, who ran away from me!

LADY H. O, how can I bear it! what a tragedy is this! To find—again—and to lose!

LIO. Before mine eyes beheld thee, my heart recognized thee—

LADY H. Recognized me? Surely you are mistaken, sir!

LIO. No! Every line of your face is graven on my heart. I cannot be wrong. It is Martha's voice that I hear. There can be no mistake.

LADY H. You are dreaming!

LIO. If this be a dream, O let me never awake from it! Ah, I would dream thus forever. Disturb not so sweet a slumber!

LADY H. O go, I beg you go!

LIO. No, no. In my dream let me take your hand, "as I did once—do you remember? Let me kiss it—thus—to tell my love.

LADY H. I can no longer tolerate such gross impertinence. Will you go, sir?

LIO. Wherefore this pretence? Why do you disown me?

LADY H. Hence, peasant clown—begone!

LIO. I, a peasant? I, your master? Patience is thrown away on you! I have been too gentle. Now I *command* you to come instantly with me! (*Takes her arm.*)

LADY H. Tristan—help, help!

(TRISTAN *comes hurrying in, afterward followed by the others.*)

TRIS. What has alarmed you? Speak!

LADY H. Help me—save me from that fellow!

TRIS. Who dares to—

LIO. My lord, this is my servant, and I have a right to take her hence.

TRIS. Listen to the brazen impudence of the fellow! It is really too horrid, don't you know? It fairly makes me shudder. The most unheard of audacity—Come here—all of you. (*Summoning the rest. They sing.*)

NO. 17.

CHO. How audacious, rude and daring,
To insult a lady so,
'Tis a scandal past declaring,
Off to jail the clown must go.

LADY H. Ah, 'tis agony and rapture,
That he loves me is too true,
I'm consenting to his capture,
O my heart, what can I do?

CHO. Insolent beyond expression
Thus upon our sports to break,
For his terrible transgression
Signal vengeance let us take.

LIO. Ah, 'tis agony and rapture,
Thus once more her face to view,
She's consenting to my capture,
Break, then, heart, what else canst do?

(PLUNKET *enters at close of chorus and sees* LIONEL *held by men. Sings.*)

PLUN. Hold! Pray tell me what this means?

LIO. Come, defend me!

(NANCY *enters from inn.*)

NAN. What's occur'd?

LIO. Betsy, too?

PLUN. Betsy, too.

NAN. Don't be afraid, my lady.

LIO. Lady? Now all is clear.
All her charm, her kindly manner
Were caprice and cruel sport
To amuse a lady's leisure hour—
O, just heaven, how harsh thou art.

LADY H. Pity for this fellow asking
His free pardon let me crave;
In his brain is madness masking,
That is why his fancies rave.

CHO. (*starting back*). Madness? Madness?

LIO. O, what falseness!

NAN. O, poor creature!

PLUN. List, I pray.

TRIS. No, no, away.

TRIS. (*speaks*). Arrest that madman!

PLUN. *and* LIO. Arrest him? Arrest me? (*He is seized.*)

LADY H. O, this is agony! (*Aside.*)

NAN. O, this is too hard! (*Aside.*)

LIO. But she agreed to it—she pledged herself.

LADY H. (*aside* to LIONEL). In the name of pity, be silent!

LIO. She accepted the earnest money. She bound herself to serve me for a year.

CHO. (*laughing and chattering suddenly*). How absurd! Ha! ha! ha! It really is too funny! (*Repeating.*)

LADY H. O, but let him be treated kindly. It is plain that the poor man is distraught. He is out of his senses. He does not know what he is saying.

LIO. O cruel, O false!

NAN. (*aside*). Poor fellow.

PLUN. (*to* LIONEL). A word with you.

TRIS. Away, varlet! (*Trumpets are heard outside.*) The Queen is approaching!

LIO. The Queen! Ah! her coming brings me hope! (*Takes ring from his finger and gives it to* PLUNKET.) This is the ring which my father left for me. He told you that if I ever should be in trouble this ring must be presented to the Queen. She will recognize it and will send me aid at once. Now is the hour which my father foresaw—O, unhappy day! Now is the hour to redeem the pledge he left with us, the pledge of his honor and mine. (*Turns to* LADY H. *and gazes at her longingly.*) As for you, how shall I bear the memory of your treachery? (*Sings.*)

NO. 18. FINALE.

LIO. Heav'n forgive this cruel scorning,
All my anguish pardon you,
You, my life's one best beloved,
Teach me hearts can prove untrue.

LADY H. Heav'n forgive my faithless heart,
Forgive my scorning,
All his anguish pardon me.

LIO. Cruel girl, does it add to your joy
To wound the heart that loves you well?
My wild grief, my deep despairing,
Must my love and madness tell.

CHO. Just rebuke of his offences,
Shall not cause so much dismay.
Off to prison let's despatch him,
So our sport no longer delay.

LADY H. Ah, I wound a heart that loves me well.

(*Curtain falls as* LIONEL *is led off under arrest, and* LADY H. *steps into a sedan chair which has been brought on. Tableau.*)

ACT FIVE.

(*Curtain rises on Richmond fair scene, set as before. The courtiers, all dressed as farmers and maid servants, are standing about.*)

NO. 18a.

CHO. I can sew, sir, I can scrub, sir,
I'm a good one at a tub, sir,
Yes, to every sort of work
My hand I turn and never shirk, etc. (*as before*).

(LADY HARRIET, NANCY *and* PLUNKET *enter and come down front while chorus sings.* LIONEL *enters from the other side and wanders about among the booths, not looking at anything or anyone, wrapped in a deep reverie. He is plainly distraught, utterly unbalanced by the sad experience he has had.* LADY H. *and* NAN. *are in their hunting costumes.*)

PLUN. Poor Lionel! He seems quite lost to me! He avoids me, seeks solitude, or if he does approach his fellow men he utterly ignores their presence, as now.

NANCY. Does he seem to have no moments when he knows you?

PLUN. Not so far. Ever since the Queen recognized the ring I gave her and restored him to his rightful place and name as Earl of Derby he seems to think he is no more himself. All the past is wiped away from his thought and he wanders about in a daze or dream.

LADY H. And I am the one who is to blame!

PLUN. Yes—and no. Nancy here did by me much what you did by Lionel, but it did not drive me crazy. So after all it is partly Lionel's strange nature that is to blame. He was always a queer lad, sensitive to a fault.

NAN. Did you really think I meant the girls to stick their spears into you? I was furious with them!

LADY H. It was my hope that if Lionel found himself again in the midst of this familiar scene where first we met he might recognize me and come to himself again.

NANCY. But not when you are in those clothes. This is the costume you wore when you were so cruel to him.

LADY H. That is true. I had forgotten, in my zeal to get all the rest of them ready. But here he comes. O, Lionel, don't you know me? (*He repulses her.*)

NO. 19.

LIO. When I first that hand did claim,
Was I not repulsed with laughter?
Did that hand not heavy chains
Heap upon me, heedless after?
No, this hand which yesterday,
But yesterday did drive me forth,
Though today 'tis kind again
Ah, to me 'tis nothing worth!

LADY H. O, he is cruel!

LIO. Love is turned to hate!
I thought her sent by heav'n to bless,
To shed around her happiness;
What deep and glowing ecstasy
Filled all my heart
When first she smiled on me!

LADY H. Oh, can these eyes, grown dim with grief,
And wan with tears, seek to betray you?
Oh, doubt me not, for I am thine.

LIO. I ne'er again can call thee mine!
Dead for aye my trust in thee
Hateful art thou grown to me!

(LIONEL *rushes of the stage.* LADY H. *sinks weeping into the arms of* NANCY.)

PLUN. Courage, my lady! I see in this very frenzy a hopeful change. His apathy and indifference were far worse. At least you waked him up. Better luck next time.

NAN. Go, my lady, and come back again in the simple little dress of Martha. When he sees you so it will call up the old memories and then—if you sing to him—surely his strange hallucination will not continue. (LADY H. *goes off.*)

PLUN. Poor lass, my heart aches for her—or it would, if it were not so busy aching for itself.

NAN. Yes, it is hardest of all for you—you have loved Lord Lionel so long.

PLUN. To tell the truth I was not thinking wholly of Lionel, either!

NAN. (*demurely*). You have troubles of your own?

PLUN. You know very well what I mean!—I shall be so lonely when he leaves me to go and live on his grand estates.—Will you think of me sometimes, Miss Nancy, sitting all alone in my poor farmhouse?

NAN. Ye-es, perhaps—I don't know. I shall think how you sit and si-i-igh—like that. (*Sighs in mock-serious fashion.*) Ah-h-h!

PLUN. You needn't laugh. It is a serious matter. I am very much to be pitied.

NAN. If you could only—(*hesitates*)

PLUN. What is she going to say now, the witch? (*Aside.*)

NAN. If you could—couldn't you get some one to come and live with you—a friend, perhaps—or even—a wife—now! Just let your imagination work a little.

PLUN. That's so, I *might* get somebody to marry me! That would be a good idea. I have a pretty neighbor—a farmer's daughter—

NAN. O, indeed! A farmer's daughter? A good steady girl, I've no doubt, who would always do exactly what you told her. That's an excellent idea. Marry her by all means!

PLUN. Will you dance at the wedding?

NAN. Certainly—and who with a lighter heart? Remember to send me an invitation.

PLUN. No, I won't, you little minx!

NAN. Won't invite me?

PLUN. Won't marry her.

NAN. Why not?

PLUN. I am not in love with her.

NAN. But you will find plenty of other handsome lasses.

PLUN. The more I search, the less I find.

NAN. O, indeed. How unfortunate—for the girls!

PLUN. None of them suit me. You see, I had a maid once—a little serving maid—the gayest, prettiest creature—but she ran away from me—

NAN. Perhaps you were not kind to her?

PLUN. Kind, I? I was kindness itself! I was *too* kind! I *killed* her with kindness!

NAN. Well, that's the trouble, then. A girl needs a good firm upstanding sort of a way, to keep her in her place. Don't be too easy,—take my advice. But tell me about your servant.

PLUN. O, I don't know as she was so much, after all. But I found her amusing. She was a well-meaning sort of creature, and rather good looking, but she couldn't do a thing! She could not knit or spin, she could only laugh and joke.—But ignorant as she was, she knew one thing.

NAN. What was that?

PLUN. How to make me miss her!

NAN. Perhaps she misses you!

PLUN. (*starts toward her*). Nancy—my little Betsy Ann!

NAN. And though she does not know the things you say, though she is a poor silly creature who never did a useful thing in all her life—could she not learn?

PLUN. Don't torment me, girl. Do you mean what you say?

NAN. (*laughing at him*). Certainly I mean it. What clever girl could not learn those things—if she really—

PLUN. Really—what?—

NAN. O, if it were worth while!

PLUN. O Nancy, is it worth while?—But no, we must not think of ourselves while Lionel is in such a state—my poor Lionel! Until he is right again my home is his.

NAN. (*walking off a little stiffly*). O, keep your old home! Nobody wants it!

PLUN. (*goes after her and speaks in her ear*). I mean to keep it—and you!

NAN. If you can!

PLUN. I can. A voice whispers in my heart!

NAN. What is the voice that whispers in your heart?

PLUN. It is the voice of love.

(LADY H. *returns in peasant costume. She goes up to the groups of farmers and begins to arrange them in the old order. Speaks.*)

LADY H. Arrange everything just as it was before. Bring the big chair for the sheriff. Don't look at Lionel. Pretend to be all occupied with the business of the day.

NAN. (*looking off*). Here he comes, with his sad and gentle look. Sing to him, my lady.

(*Music begins with* NANCY'S *speech.* LADY H. *sings.*)

NO. 20.

LADY H. Now the April day returning
Girds the earth with living green;
As the moon shines clearer, fairer,
Spring's new loveliness is seen.
Laughing flowers that gem the meadows,
With the stars in beauty vie,
While the nightingale with singing,
Tells his love to earth and sky.

LIO. Heaven! Martha's singing!

LADY H. (*approaches him timidly*). See, 'tis Martha.

CHO. See, he knows her! Sadly, but mildly
Meets her glances
And our advances.

(LIONEL *moves about among the supposed servants in wonderment.*)

(NANCY *steps from among them.*)

NAN. Now hither troop both young and old
The village clock the hour has told!
I can darn, sir, I can sew, sir,
I can milk and I can mow, sir,
I can bake and mend and make,
And garden beds can hoe and rake.

CHO. Yes, I can clean, sir, I can scrub, sir,
I'm a good one at the tub, sir (*etc., as before*).

PLUN. (*to* LIONEL). Come, this way,
We'll choose a servant;
Come with me.

LIO. (*passes his hand over his brow in bewilderment*).O, what is it?

PLUN. Why, the servants
Who at Richmond market gather.
Come, then, choose which one you'd rather.

(*They approach* LADY HARRIET *and* NANCY. LIONEL *stands and gazes at* LADY H. *He speaks.*)

LIO. (*perplexed*). Martha, Martha! Is it you? Tell me that this is indeed you! Tell me that it is no dream. We are together at last!

LADY H. Lionel, I am Martha, and your humble, loving servant. You know what has come to you, fortune and a splendid name. But before I knew of this, my heart repented. I was ready to go to you in your prison and claim you as my love. Then you were set free without my aid—O wretched, cruel girl that I was! Lionel, I am fairly punished for my worldly pride, my cruel impulse. But life is hard for girls. Think how they might all have scorned me if I confessed to having been a servant! But now I care for nothing—only you.

LIO. Let all the past be forgotten. Joy smiles at last. At last my dreams have all come true.

PLUN. (*to* NANCY). And what can you do, you useless bit of baggage?

NANCY (*hums*). I can cook, sir, I can bake, sir,—

PLUN. (*laughing*). You are jesting. You are my own little good-for-nothing.

NAN. If my master is obstinate—I can bring him to reason.

PLUN. You will suit me, after all. You will make an excellent farmer's wife. Come along.

NAN. There! (*She boxes his ear.*) Take that as an earnest.

LADY H. *sings.*

NO. 21. FINALE.

LADY H. Now the April days returning
Gird the Spring in living green.

LIO. As the moon shines clearer, fairer,
Spring's new loveliness is seen.

LADY H. *and* LIO. While the nightingale with singing,
Tells his love to earth and sky,
Sounds at last love's hour of promise,
Hour of hope and nuptial joy.

CHO. Sounds at last love's hour of promise,
Hour of hope and nuptial joy.

Curtain.

END.

CPSIA information can be obtained
at www.ICGtesting.com
Printed in the USA
LVHW100714050223
738616LV00026B/1185

9 789356 909724